REALLY EASY GUITAR

ACOUSTIC CLASSICS

22 SONGS WITH CHORDS, LYRICS & BASIC TAB

ISBN 978-1-5400-6307-6

Visit Hal Leonard Online at
www.halleonard.com

Contact us:
Hal Leonard
7777 West Bluemound Road
Milwaukee, WI 53213
Email: info@halleonard.com

In Europe, contact:
Hal Leonard Europe Limited
42 Wigmore Street
Marylebone, London, W1U 2RN
Email: info@halleonardeurope.com

In Australia, contact:
Hal Leonard Australia Pty. Ltd.
4 Lentara Court
Cheltenham, Victoria, 3192 Australia
Email: info@halleonard.com.au

GUITAR NOTATION LEGEND

Chord Diagrams

CHORD DIAGRAMS graphically represent the guitar fretboard to show correct chord fingerings.

• The letter above the diagram tells the name of the chord.

• The top, bold horizontal line represents the nut of the guitar. Each thin horizontal line represents a fret. Each vertical line represents a string; the low E string is on the far left and the high E string is on the far right.

• A dot shows where to put your fret-hand finger and the number at the bottom of the diagram tells which finger to use.

• The "O" above the string means play it open, while an "X" means don't play the string.

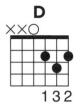

Tablature

TABLATURE graphically represents the guitar fingerboard. Each horizontal line represents a string, and each number represents a fret.

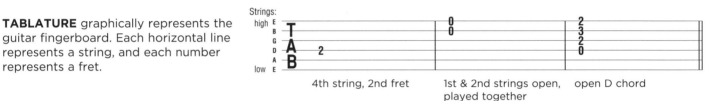

4th string, 2nd fret   1st & 2nd strings open, played together   open D chord

Definitions for Special Guitar Notation

HAMMER-ON: Strike the first (lower) note with one finger, then sound the higher note (on the same string) with another finger by fretting it without picking.

PULL-OFF: Place both fingers on the notes to be sounded. Strike the first note and without picking, pull the finger off to sound the second (lower) note.

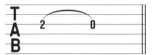

LEGATO SLIDE: Strike the first note and then slide the same fret-hand finger up or down to the second note. The second note is not struck.

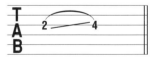

SHIFT SLIDE: Same as legato slide, except the second note is struck.

Additional Musical Definitions

N.C.   • No chord. Instrument is silent.

• Repeat measures between signs.

Angie

Words and Music by Mick Jagger and Keith Richards

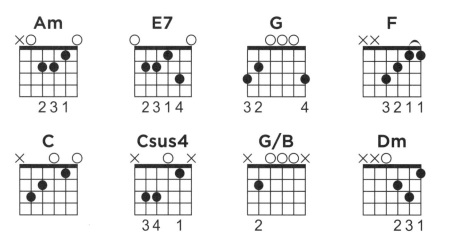

INTRO

Moderately

| Am | E7 | G   F | Csus4   C   G/B ‖

VERSE 1

Am   E7   G   F   Csus4   C   G/B
    Angie,   Angie,   when will those clouds all disappear?

Am   E7   G   F   Csus4   C
    Angie, Angie,   where will it lead us from here?

       G   Dm   Am   C   F   G
With no lovin' in our souls and no money in our coats,   you can't say we're satisfied.

Am   E7   G   F   Csus4   C   G/B
Angie, Angie,   you can't say we never tried.

VERSE 2

Am   E7   G   F   Csus4   C   G/B
    Angie, you're beautiful,   but ain't it time we said goodbye?

Am   E7   G   F   Csus4   C
    Angie,   I still love ya.   Remember all those nights we cried?

       G   Dm   Am
All the dreams we held so close seemed to all go up in smoke,

C   F   G
    uh, let me whisper in your ear.

Am   E7   G   F   Csus4   C   G/B
Angie, Angie,   where will it lead us from here?

INTERLUDE 1

| Am | E7 | G F | Csus4 C G/B |

| Am | E7 | G F | Csus4 C |

VERSE 3

    G   Dm   Am C   F   G
Oh, Angie, don't you weep, all your kisses still taste sweet.   I hate that sadness in your eyes.

    Am   E7   G   F   Csus4 C G/B
But Angie, Angie,   ain't it time we said goodbye?

INTERLUDE 2

| Am | E7 | G F | Csus4 C |

BRIDGE

      G   Dm   Am C   F   G
With no lovin' in our souls and no money in our coats,   you can't say we're satisfied.

    Dm   Am Dm   Am
But Angie, I still love you, baby.   Ev'rywhere I look I see your eyes.

Dm   Am   C   F   G
    There ain't a woman that comes close to you,   come on, baby, dry your eyes.

OUTRO

    Am   E7   G   F   Csus4 C G/B
Angie, Angie,   ain't it good to be alive?

    Am   E7   G   F   Csus4 C
    Angie, Angie,   we can't say we never tried.

Babe, I'm Gonna Leave You

Words and Music by Anne Bredon, Jimmy Page and Robert Plant

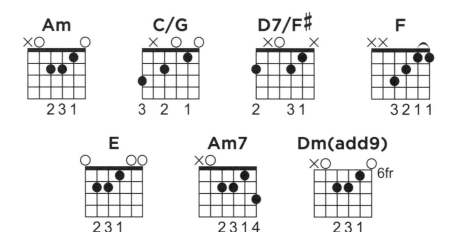

INTRO

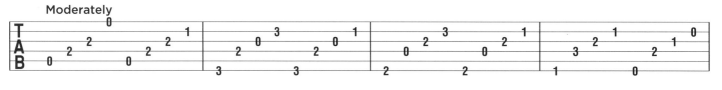

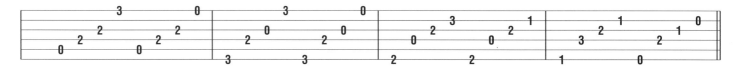

VERSE 1

Am   C/G D7/F#   F E
Babe,   baby,   baby,

    Am   C/G   D7/F#   F E
I'm gonna leave you.

       Am   C/G   D7/F# F   E
I said,   baby,   you know

    Am   C/G   D7/F# F E
I'm gonna leave you.

    F   E   F   E
I'll leave you when the summer time,   leave you when the summer comes

Am   C/G   D7/F#   F   E
a rollin',   leave you when the summer   comes

INTERLUDE 1

Play 3 times

Am   Am7 Dm(add9)| ||: Am   Am7 Dm(add9)| :||
along.

VERSE 2

Am   C/G   D7/F♯   F   E
Babe, babe, babe, babe, babe, babe, baby, mm,   baby,

Am   C/G   D7/F♯   F   E
I wanna leave you.   I ain't jokin',   woman, I've got to

Am   C/G   D7/F♯   F   E
ramble.   Oh, yeah.

Am   C/G   D7/F♯   F   E
Baby, baby, I will leave you. I've really   got to

F   E   F   E
ramble.   I can hear it callin' me the way it

Am   C/G   D7/F♯   F   E
used to do.   I can hear it callin' me   back home.

INTERLUDE 2

Play 3 times

| Am   Am7   Dm(add9) | ‖: Am   Am7   Dm(add9) :‖
whoa.

Play 3 times

VERSE 3

Am   C/G   D7/F♯   F   E
Baby,   oh,   babe,

              Am   C/G   D7/F♯   F   E
I'm gonna leave you.   Oh,

Am   C/G   D7/F♯   F   E
ba -   by,   you know   I've really

Am   C/G   D7/F♯   F   E
got to leave you.   Oh.

F   E   F   E
I could hear it callin' me,   I said, "Don't you hear it   callin' me the way it

INTERLUDE 2

Play 3 times

| Am   Am7   Dm(add9) | ‖: Am   Am7   Dm(add9) :‖
used to do?"

REPEAT INTRO

VERSE 4

Am   C/G   D7/F♯   F   E
I know,   I know,   I know I never, never, never, never, never gonna

Am   C/G   D7/F♯   F   E
leave you, babe,   but I gotta go away from this place.

Am   C/G   D7/F♯   F   E
      I gotta quit you, yeah.   Oh,

Am   C/G   D7/F♯   F   E
baby,   baby, baby,   baby,

Am   C/G   D7/F♯   F   E
baby,   baby,   baby,   oh.

Am   C/G   D7/F♯   F   E
     Don't you hear it callin' me?

VERSE 5

Am   C/G   D7/F♯   F   E
     Oh,   woman,

Am   C/G   D7/F♯   F   E
   woman,   I know,   I know,

     Am   C/G   D7/F♯   F   E
feels good to have you back again and I know that one day, baby, it's gonna

     Am   C/G   D7/F♯   F   E
really grow, yes, it is.   We gonna go walkin' through the park ev'ry day.

Am   C/G   D7/F♯   F   E
     Oh my babe,   every day.   Oh.

Am   C/G   D7/F♯   F   E
   My, my,   my, my,   my, my, babe.   I'm gonna leave you,

VERSE 6

Am   C/G   D7/F♯   F   E
go away.   Oh.

Am   C/G   D7/F♯   F   E

    Am   C/G   D7/F♯   F   E
So good, sweet baby.   It was really,

Am   C/G   D7/F♯   F   E
   really good.   You made me happy ev'ry   single

Am   C/G   D7/F♯   F   E
day,   but now   I've got to go

  Am   C/G   D7/F♯   F   E
away.   Oh,   oh,

Am   C/G   D7/F♯   F   E
oh.

Am   C/G   D7/F♯   F   E
(Oo.

Am   C/G   D7/F♯   F   E
Oo.)   Baby,   baby,   baby

OUTRO

F   E

that's when it's callin' me.

F   E

I said, that's when it's callin' me back home.

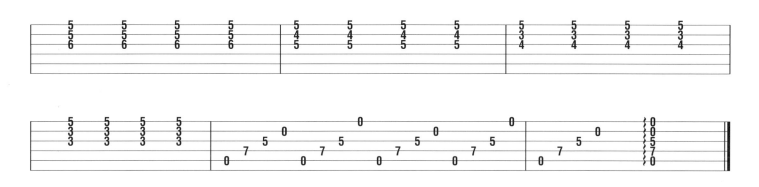

Behind Blue Eyes

Words and Music by Peter Townshend

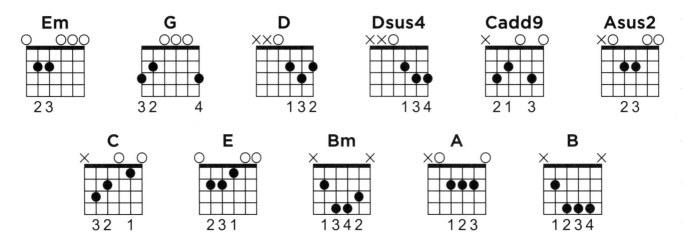

INTRO

Moderately

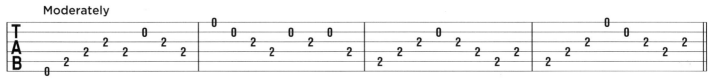

VERSE 1

```
Em                    G       D    Dsus4  D
No one knows what it's like to be the bad man,

     Cadd9      Asus2
to be the sad man behind blue eyes.

Em                    G       D    Dsus4  D
No one knows what it's like to be hated,

     Cadd9      Asus2
to be fated to telling only lies.
```

CHORUS

```
     C      D          G
But my dreams,   they aren't as empty

     C      D        E
as my conscience seems to be.

     Bm         C
I have hours only lonely.

     D                Asus2
My love is vengeance that's never free.
```

VERSE 2

```
Em                        G            D     Dsus4  D
No one knows what it's like to feel these feelings
        Cadd9              Asus2
like I do,     and I blame you.
Em                        G            D     Dsus4  D
No one bites back as hard on their anger.
        Cadd9              Asus2
None of my pain and woe can show through.
```

REPEAT CHORUS

INTERLUDE 1

```
| E            Bm |        A      E |              Bm |        A
```

BRIDGE

```
  E           Bm      A        E        Bm      G    D
   When my fist clenches, crack it open    before I use it and lose my cool.
        Bm   A          D           Bm   A        E    Bm   A
When I smile, tell me some bad news before I laugh and act like a    fool.
  E     Bm    A       E           Bm   G       D
   And if I swallow anything evil, put your finger down my    throat.
        Bm        A        D           Bm        A
And if I shiver, please,    give me a blanket, keep me warm, let me wear your coat.
```

INTERLUDE 2

```
| E            Bm |      A      E  |              Bm |      A        B  |
                           Play 3 times
||: B        A   |   G    D      B  :||               |                 ||
```

OUTRO

```
Em                        G            D     Dsus4  D
No one knows what it's like to be the bad man,
        Cadd9       Asus2
to be the sad man behind blue eyes.
```

Best of My Love

Words and Music by Don Henley, Glenn Frey and John David Souther

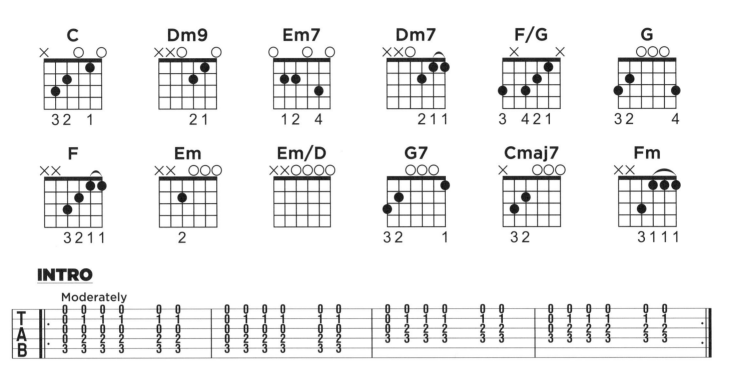

INTRO

Moderately

VERSE 1

C   Dm9
Every night I'm lyin' in bed holdin' you close in my dreams.

C   Dm9
Thinkin' about all the things that we said and comin' apart at the seams.

Em7   Dm7   Em7   F/G
We tried to talk it o - ver but the words come out too rough.

C   Dm9   C   G F Em Em/D
I know you were tryin' to give me the best of your love.

VERSE 2

C   Dm9
Beautiful faces and loud empty places,   look at the way we live.

C   Dm9
Wastin' our time on cheap talk and wine   left us so little to give.

Em7   Dm7   Em7   Dm7 G7
That same old crowd was like a cold, dark cloud that we could never rise above.

C   Dm9   C   G F Em Em/D
But here in my heart, I give you the best of my love.   (Whoa,

CHORUS 1

C   Dm7
       You get the best of my love.
  sweet darlin',   you get the best of my love. Whoa,
C   Dm7
       You get the best of my love.
  sweet darlin',   you get the best of my love.)

BRIDGE

Fm   Cmaj7
   I'm goin' back in time and it's a sweet dream.

      Fm   Dm7 G
It was a quiet night, and I would be alright if I could go on sleeping.

VERSE 3

     C   Dm9
But every morning I wake up and worry   what's gonna happen today.

C   Dm9
You see it your way and I see it mine, but we both see it slippin' away.

Em7   Dm7 Em7   Dm7 G7
   You know we always had each other, baby.   I guess that wasn't enough.   Oh, oh

    C   Dm9   C   G F Em Em/D
but here in my heart, I give you the best of my love.   (Whoa,

CHORUS 2

C   Dm7
                The best of my
  sweet darlin',   you get the best of my love.   Whoa,
C   Dm7
love.   The best of my
   sweet darlin',   you get the best of my love.   Whoa,
C   Dm7
love.   Every night and day.   The best of my
  sweet darlin',   you get the best of my love.   Whoa,
C   Dm7
love.   Oh, oh.   The best of my
  sweet darlin',   you get the best of my love.   Whoa,
C   Dm7
love.   You get the best of my love.   The best of my
  sweet darlin',   you get the best of my love.   Whoa,
C   Dm7   C   *Fade out*
love.   Oo.   The best of my love.
  sweet darlin',   you get the best of my love. Whoa,   sweet darlin '.)

Blackbird

Words and Music John Lennon and Paul McCartney

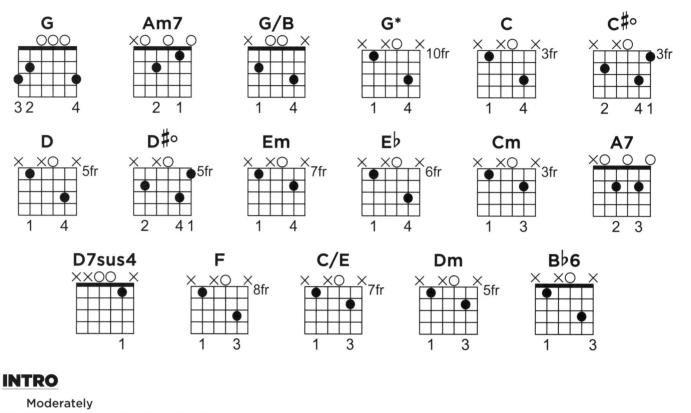

INTRO

Moderately

w/ fingers

VERSE 1

```
G        Am7      G/B  G*
Blackbird singing in the dead of night,

C        C#°          D    D#°    Em    Eb
take these broken wings    and learn to fly.

D     C#°   C    Cm
All your life,

G/B              A7        D7sus4         G
you were only waiting for this moment to arise.
```

INTERLUDE 1

VERSE 2

G   Am7   G/B   G*
Blackbird singing in the dead of night,

C   C#o   D   D#o   Em   E♭
take these sunken eyes   and learn to see.

D   C#o   C   Cm
All your life,

G/B   A7   D7sus4   G
you were only waiting for this moment to to be free.

BRIDGE

F C/E Dm C B♭6 C
Black - bird   fly,

F C/E Dm C B♭6 A7   D7sus4
Black - bird   fly,   into the light of the dark black

INTERLUDE 2

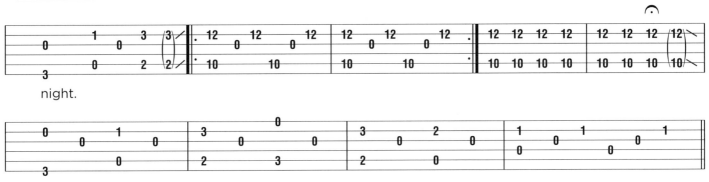

night.

REPEAT BRIDGE

INTERLUDE 3

night.

REPEAT VERSE 1

OUTRO

C	G/B	A7	D7sus4	G

You were only waiting for this moment to arise.

C	G/B	A7	D7sus4	G

You were only waiting for this moment to arise.

C	G/B	A7	D7sus4	G

You were only waiting for this moment to arise.

More Than a Feeling

Words and Music by Tom Scholz

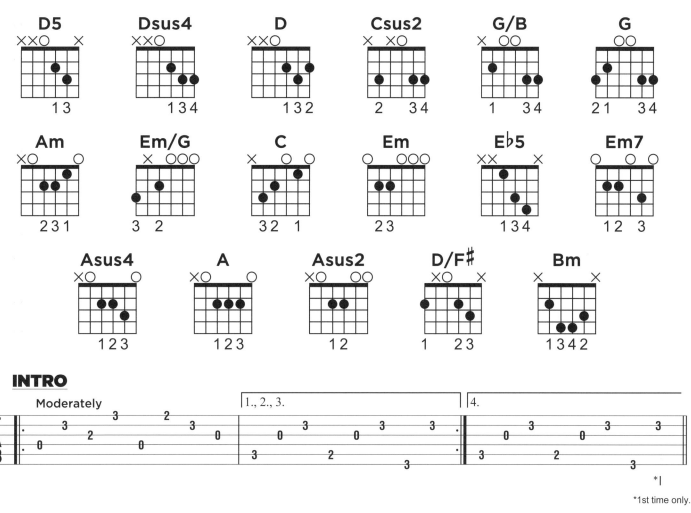

INTRO

Moderately

1., 2., 3.

4.

*1

*1st time only.

VERSE 1

| D5 | | Dsus4 D | Csus2 | | G/B G |
looked out this morn - ing and the sun was gone,

| D5 | | Dsus4 D | Csus2 | G/B G |
turned on some mu - sic to start my day.

| D5 | Dsus4 D | | Csus2 | G/B G |
I lost myself in a familiar song.

| D5 | | Dsus4 D | Csus2 | | G/B Am | Em/G D Dsus4 |
I closed my eyes and I slipped away.

INTERLUDE 1

| G   C | Em   D C | G   C | Em   D |

CHORUS 1

```
    G           C    Em         D    G              C         Em            D
It's more than a feeling                when I hear that old song   they used to     play.
                (More than a feeling.                               More than a feeling.
    G           C    Em         D   G          C        E♭5
And I begin dreaming            till I see Marianne    walk away.
                   More than a feeling.)
Em7             Asus4  A   Asus2       A      G   D/F♯  Em7
    I see my Mar  -   ianne        walkin' away.
```

INTERLUDE 2

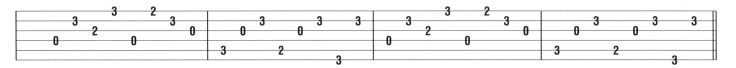

VERSE 2

```
    D5      Dsus4  D  Csus2      G/B  G
So many people   have come and gone,

    D5   Dsus4  D      Csus2  G/B  G
their faces fade    as the years   go by.

    D5      Dsus4  D  Csus2  G/B  G
Yet I still recall        as I wander on,

    D5        Dsus4  D  Csus2        G/B  Am  Em/G  D  Dsus4
as clear as the sun        in the summer sky.
```

REPEAT INTERLUDE 1

CHORUS 2

```
    G           C    Em         D    G              C         Em            D
It's more than a feeling                when I hear that old song   they used to     play.
                (More than a feeling.                               More than a feeling.
    G           C    Em         D   G          C        E♭5
And I begin dreaming            till I see Marianne    walk away.
                   More than a feeling.)
Em7             Asus4  A   Asus2       A      Bm  A  G  D/F♯  Asus4   A
    I see my Mar  -   ianne        walkin' away.
```

GUITAR SOLO

```
                  1., 2.              3.
‖: D      G    | D/F♯    A    :‖ Bm    A    |  D      Bm   | Em7    A    |  G             |    D/F♯  Em7 ‖
```

INTERLUDE 3

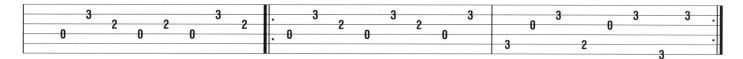

VERSE 3

D5   Dsus4 D   Csus2 G/B G
When I'm tired   and thinking cold,

D5   Dsus4 D   Csus2 G/B G
I hide in my mu - sic, forget the day

D5   Dsus4 D Csus2   G/B G
and dream of a girl   I used to know.

D5   Dsus4 D   Csus2 G/B Csus2
I closed my eyes   and she slipped away.

D5 Dsus4 D Csus2 G/B Csus2

D5 Dsus4 D Csus2 G/B   Csus2
                        She slipped away.

D5 Dsus4 D Csus2 G/B Csus2

D5 Dsus4 D Csus2 G/B Am Em/G D

REPEAT INTERLUDE 1

CHORUS 3

G   C Em   D G   C   Em   D
It's more than a feeling   when I hear that old song   they used to   play.
                  (More than a feeling.   More than a feeling.

G   C Em   D G   C   Em D
And I begin dreaming   till I see Marianne   walk away.
                More than a feeling.)

OUTRO

Repeat and fade

‖: G   C | Em   D   :‖

Dust in the Wind

Words and Music by Kerry Livgren

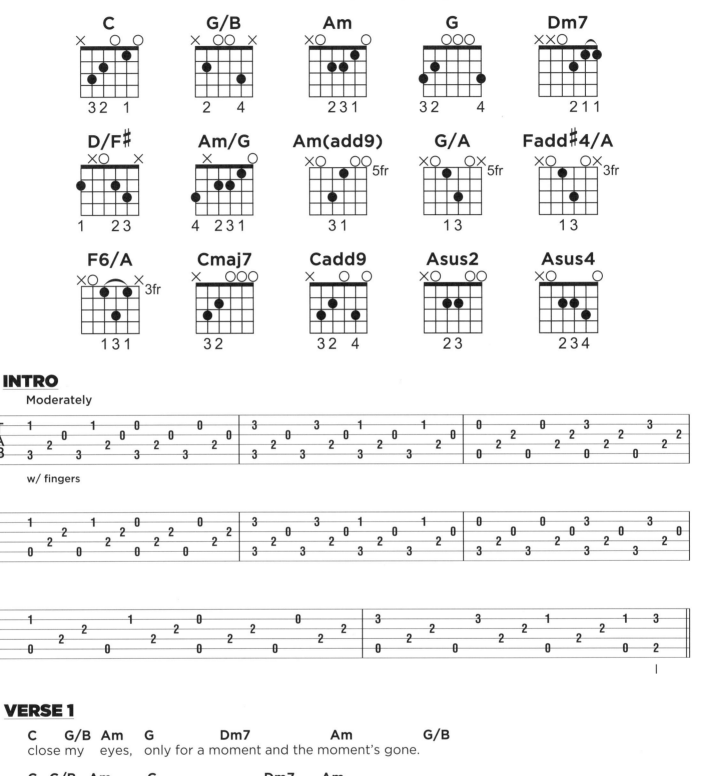

INTRO

Moderately

w/ fingers

VERSE 1

C G/B Am   G   Dm7   Am   G/B
close my   eyes,   only for a moment and the moment's gone.

C G/B Am   G   Dm7   Am
All my   dreams   pass before my eyes, a curiosity.

CHORUS 1

D/F#   G   Am   Am/G
      Dust   in the wind.

D/F#   G   Am G/B
All they are is dust in the wind

VERSE 2

```
C    G/B  Am   G              Dm7       Am       G/B
Same old   song,   just a drop of water in an endless sea.
```

```
 C  G/B  Am   G              Dm7               Am
All we    do    crumbles to the ground though we refuse to see.
```

CHORUS 2

```
D/F♯      G        Am    Am/G
   Dust    in the wind.
```

```
D/F♯       G         Am(add9)   G/A    Fadd♯4/A    F6/A  Fadd♯4/A
All we are is dust in the wind.         Oh,        ho, ho.
```

INTERLUDE 1

```
‖: Am(add9)        | G/A              | Fadd♯4/A        | F6/A       Fadd♯4/A :‖

| C       Cmaj7   | Cadd9    C        | Asus2    Asus4  | Am         Asus2      |

| Cadd9   C       | Cmaj7    Cadd9    | Am       Asus2  | Asus4   Am    G/B  ‖
                                                                      Now,
```

VERSE 3

```
C    G/B  Am   G              Dm7       Am       G/B
Don't hang  on,    nothing lasts forever but the earth and sky. It
```

```
C    G/B  Am   G              Dm7               Am
slips a  -   way and all your money won't another minute buy.
```

CHORUS 3

```
D/F♯      G        Am    Am/G
   Dust    in the wind.
```

```
D/F♯       G        Am              Am/G
All we are is dust in the wind.
                              (All we are is dust in the
```

```
D/F♯       G        Am              Am/G
   Dust    in the wind.
wind.               Everything is dust in the
```

```
D/F♯       G
Everything is dust in the
wind.)
```

OUTRO

```
| Am        Asus2    | Asus4     Am     | Asus2      Asus4        |
 wind                                The       wind    Repeat and fade

‖: Am        Asus2    | Asus4     Am     | Asus2      Asus4      :‖
```

Fire and Rain

Words and Music by James Taylor

(Capo 3rd Fret)

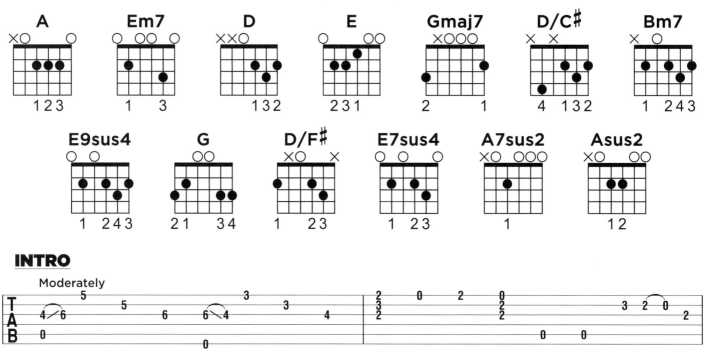

INTRO

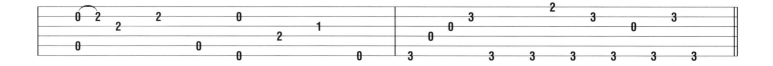

VERSE 1

A   Em7   D   A
Just yesterday mornin', they let me know you were gone.

E   Gmaj7
Suzanne, the plans they made put an end to you.

A   Em7   D   A
I walked out this morning and I wrote down this song.

E   Gmaj7
I just can't remember who to send it to.

CHORUS 1

D   D/C#   Bm7   E9sus4   A
I've seen fire and I've seen rain.

D   D/C#   Bm7   E9sus4   A
I've seen   sunny days that I thought would never   end.

D   D/C#   Bm7   E9sus4   A
I've seen lonely times when I could not find a   friend.

G   D/F#   E7sus4   Em7   A7sus2   Asus2
But I always thought that I'd see you   again.

VERSE 2

     A   Em7   D   A
Won't you look down upon me, Jesus, you got to help me make a stand.

         E   Gmaj7
You've just got to see me through another day.

A   Em7   D   A
 My body's aching and my time is at hand.

      E   Gmaj7
 I won't make it any other way.

REPEAT CHORUS 1

VERSE 3

     A   Em7   D   A
Been walking my mind to an easy time, my back turned towards the sun.

        E   Gmaj7
Lord knows when the cold wind blows, it'll turn your head around.

     A   Em7   D   A
Well, there's hours of time on the telephone line to talk about things to come,

      E   Gmaj7
 sweet dreams and flying machines in pieces on the ground.

CHORUS 2

D D/C# Bm7 E9sus4 A
Whoa, I've seen fire and I've seen rain.

   D   D/C#   Bm7   E9sus4 A
I've seen sunny days that I thought would never end.

   D   D/C#   Bm7 E9sus4 A   A
I've seen lonely times when I could not find a friend.

  G   D/F#   E7sus4 Em7 A7sus2   Asus2
But I always thought that I'd see you, baby,   one more time again, now.

OUTRO

     A7sus2   Asus2
Thought I'd see you one more time again.

     A7sus2   Asus2
There's just a few things coming my way this time around, now.

     A7sus2   Asus2
Thought I'd see you, thought I'd see you, fire and rain, now. Na, na, na.

                             Fade

A7sus2   Asus2
 Na, na, na, na, na, na, na, na, na,   na. Na, na, na, na, na, na, na, na.

Have You Ever Seen the Rain?

Words and Music by John Fogerty

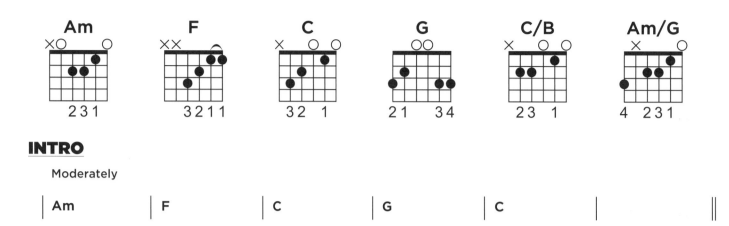

INTRO

Moderately

| Am | F | C | G | C | |

VERSE 1

C
Someone told me long ago,

                                         G
there's a calm before the storm. I know;

                 C
it's been comin' for some time.

When it's over, so they say,

                 G
it'll rain a sunny day. I know;

             C
shinin' down like water.

CHORUS

F   G   C   C/B Am Am/G
I want to know, have you ever seen the rain?

F   G   C   C/B Am Am/G
I want to know, have you ever seen the rain

F   G   C
comin' down a sunny day?

VERSE 2

C
Yesterday and days before,

                                               G
sun is cold and rain is hard. I know;

                     C
been that way for all my time.

Till forever, on it goes,

                                              G
through the circle, fast and slow. I know;

               C
it can't stop, I wonder.

CHORUS 2

F   G   C   C/B   Am   Am/G
I want to know, have you ever seen the rain?

F   G   C   C/B   Am   Am/G
I want to know, have you ever seen the rain

F   G   C
comin' down a sunny day? Yeah.

CHORUS 3

F   G   C   C/B   Am   Am/G
I want to know, have you ever seen the rain?

F   G   C   C/B   Am   Am/G
I want to know, have you ever seen the rain

F   G   C   G   C
comin' down a sunny day?

Hey You

Words and Music by Roger Waters

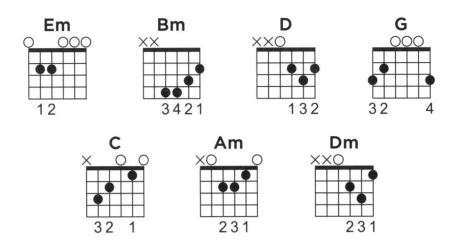

INTRO

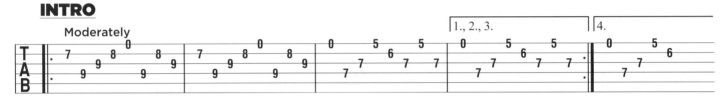

VERSE 1

Em
Hey you, out there in the cold, getting lonely, getting old, can you feel me? **Bm**

Em
Hey you, standing in the aisles with itchy feet and fading smiles, can you feel me? **Bm**

D   **G** **D** **C**
  Hey you, don't help them to bury the light.

Bm   **Am**   **Em** **Dm**
  Don't give in   without a fight.

VERSE 2

Em   **Bm**
Hey you, out there on your own, sitting naked by the phone, would you touch me?

Em   **Bm**
Hey you, with your ear against the wall, waiting for someone to call out, would you touch me?

D   **G** **D** **C**
  Hey you, would you help me to carry the stone?

Bm   **Am**   **Em**
Open your heart,   I'm comin' home.

GUITAR SOLO

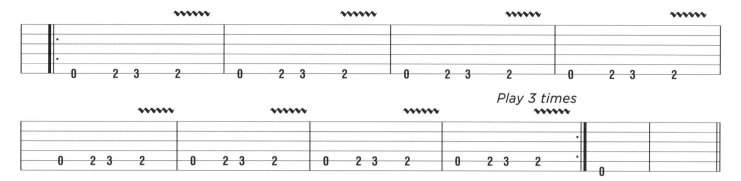

Play 3 times

BRIDGE

C   D G D C
But it was only fantasy.

                          D   G   D   C
The wall was too high as you can see.

                          D   G   D   C
No matter how he tried, he could not break free,

                          D
and the worms ate into his

INTERLUDE

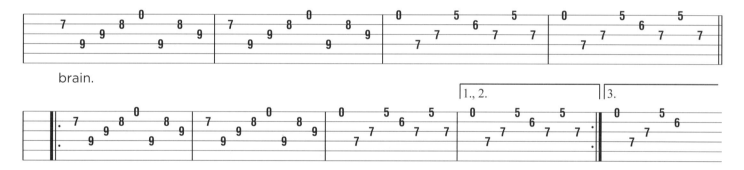

brain.

VERSE 3

       Em   Bm
Hey you, out there on the road, always doing what you're told, can you help me?

       Em   Bm
Hey you, out there beyond the wall, breaking bottles in the hall, can you help me?

D   G   D   C
Hey you, don't tell me there's no hope at all

Bm   Am   Em
Together we stand,   divided we fall.

A Horse with No Name

Words and Music by Dewey Bunnell

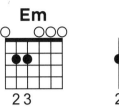

INTRO

Moderately

| Em | D⁶₉/F♯ | Em | D⁶₉/F♯ |

VERSE 1

Em   **D⁶₉/F♯**   **Em**   **D⁶₉/F♯**
On the first part of the journey I was lookin' at all the life.

Em   **D⁶₉/F♯**   **Em**   **D⁶₉/F♯**
There were plants and birds and rocks and things, there was sand and hills and rains.

Em   **D⁶₉/F♯**   **Em**   **D⁶₉/F♯**
The first thing I met was a fly with a buzz and the sky with no clouds.

Em   **D⁶₉/F♯**   **Em**   **D⁶₉/F♯**
The heat was hot and the ground was dry, but the air was full of sounds.

CHORUS 1

Em   **D⁶₉/F♯**   **Em**   **D⁶₉/F♯**
I've been through the desert on a horse with no name. It felt good to be out of the rain.

Em   **D⁶₉/F♯**   **Em**   **D⁶₉/F♯**
In the desert you can remember your name because there ain't no one for to give you no pain.

Em   **D⁶₉/F♯**   **Em**   **D⁶₉/F♯**
La, la, la,   la, la, la, la, la, la, la, la.

Em   **D⁶₉/F♯**   **Em**   **D⁶₉/F♯**
La, la, la,   la, la, la, la, la, la, la, la.

VERSE 2

Em   **D⁶₉/F♯**   **Em**   **D⁶₉/F♯**
After two days in the desert sun my skin began to turn red.

Em   **D⁶₉/F♯**   **Em**   **D⁶₉/F♯**
After three days in the desert fun I was lookin' at a riverbed.

Em   **D⁶₉/F♯**   **Em**   **D⁶₉/F♯**
And the story it told of a river that flowed, made me sad to think it was dead.

CHORUS 2

        Em   **D$_9^6$/F#**   **Em**   **D$_9^6$/F#**
You see, I've been through the desert on a horse with no name. It felt good to be out of the rain.

      Em   **D$_9^6$/F#**   **Em**   **D$_9^6$/F#**
In the desert you can remember your name 'cause there ain't no one for to give you no pain.

      Em   **D$_9^6$/F#**   **Em**   **D$_9^6$/F#**
La, la, la, la,   la, la, la, la, la, la, la, la.

      Em   **D$_9^6$/F#**   **Em**   **D$_9^6$/F#**
La, la, la, la,   la, la, la, la, la, la, la, la.

GUITAR SOLO

‖: **Em** | **D$_9^6$/F#** | **Em** | **D$_9^6$/F#**   :‖ **D$_9^6$/F#**

1.   2.

VERSE 3

      Em   **D$_9^6$/F#**   **Em**   **D$_9^6$/F#**
After nine days I let the horse run free 'cause the desert had turned to sea.

        Em   **D$_9^6$/F#**   **Em**   **D$_9^6$/F#**
There were plants and birds and rocks and things, there was sand and hills and rains.

      Em   **D$_9^6$/F#**   **Em**   **D$_9^6$/F#**
The ocean is a desert with its life underground and the perfect disguise above.

      Em   **D$_9^6$/F#**   **Em**   **D$_9^6$/F#**
Under the cities lies a heart made of ground, but the humans will give no love.

REPEAT CHORUS 2

OUTRO

      Em   **D$_9^6$/F#**   **Em**   **D$_9^6$/F#**
La, la, la, la,   la, la, la, la, la, la, la, la.

      Em   **D$_9^6$/F#**   **Em**   **D$_9^6$/F#**
La, la, la, la,   la, la, la, la, la, la, la, la.

Em   **D$_9^6$/F#**   **Em**   **D$_9^6$/F#**
La, la, la,   la, la, la, la, la, la, la.

      Em   **D$_9^6$/F#**   **Em**   **D$_9^6$/F#**
La, la, la, la,   la, la, la, la, la, la, la, la.

Em   **D$_9^6$/F#**   **Em**   **D$_9^6$/F#**
La, la, la,   la, la, la, la, la, la, la.   *Fade*

      Em   **D$_9^6$/F#**   **Em**   **D$_9^6$/F#**
La, la, la, la,   la, la, la, la, la, la, la, la.

Layla

Words and Music by Eric Clapton and Jim Gordon

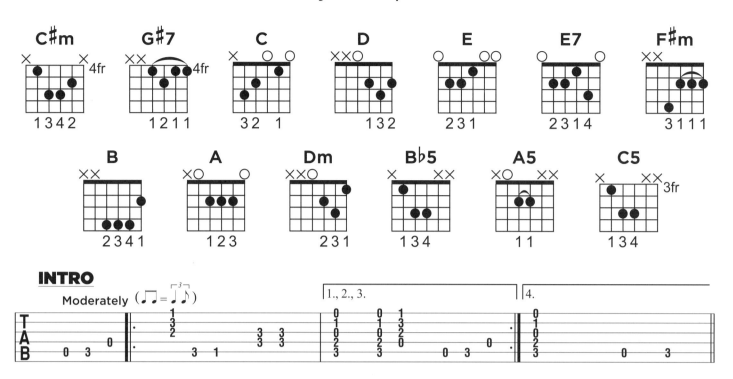

INTRODUCTION

Moderately

VERSE 1

C#m   G#7   C#m   C   D   E   E7

What will you do when you get lonely?   No one waiting by your side.

F#m   B   E   A   F#m   B   E

You've been runnin', hidin' much too long.   You know it's just your foolish pride.

CHORUS 1

A   Dm   Bb5   C   Dm

Layla,   got me on my knees.

        Bb5   C   Dm

Layla,   beggin', darlin', please.

        Bb5   C   Dm

Layla,   darlin', won't you ease my worried

      Bb5   C   A5   C5

mind?

VERSE 2

C#m   G#7   C#m   C   D   E   E7

Tried to give you consolation,   your old man, he let you down.

F#m   B   E   A   F#m   B   E

Like a fool, I fell in love with you.   You turned my whole world upside down.

REPEAT CHORUS 1

VERSE 3

C#m   G#7   C#m   C   D   E   E7
Make the best of the situation,   before I finally go insane.

F#m   B   E   A   F#m   B   E
Please don't say we'll never find a way,   tell me all my love's in vain.

CHORUS 2

A   Dm   B♭5   C   Dm
Layla,   got me on my knees.

       B♭5   C   Dm
Layla,   beggin', darlin', please.

       B♭5   C   Dm
Layla,   darlin', won't you ease my worried

       B♭5   C   Dm
mind?

CHORUS 3

Dm   B♭5   C   Dm
Layla,   got me on my knees.

       B♭5   C   Dm
Layla,   beggin', darlin', please.

       B♭5   C   Dm
Layla,   darlin', won't you ease my worried

       B♭5   C   Dm
mind?

Guitar Solo

		1.-7.		8.	
‖: Dm	B♭5	C	Dm :‖	C	Dm

REPEAT CHORUS 3

OUTRO - CHORUS

Dm   B♭5   C   Dm
Layla,   got me on my knees.

       B♭5   C   Dm
Layla,   beggin', darlin', please.

       B♭5   C   Dm
Layla,   darlin', won't you ease my worried mind?

Learning to Fly

Words and Music by Tom Petty and Jeff Lynne

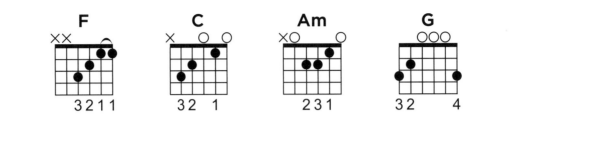

INTRO

Moderately

‖: F   C | 1., 2., 3. Am   G   :‖ | 4. Am   G

VERSE 1

F   C   Am   G   F   C   Am   G
Well, I started out   down a dirty road,

F   C   Am   G   F   C   Am   G
started out   all alone.

F   C   Am   G   F   C   Am   G
And the sun went down   as I crossed the hill.

F   C   Am   G   F   C   Am   G
And the town lit up,   the world got still.

CHORUS 1

F   C   Am   G   F   C   Am   G
I'm learning to fly   but I ain't got wings.

F   C   Am   G   F   C   Am   G
Coming down   is the hardest thing.

VERSE 2

F   C   Am   G   F   C   Am   G
Well, the good old days   may not return

F   C   Am   G   F   C   Am   G
and the rocks might melt   and the sea may burn.

CHORUS 2

F   C   Am   G   F   C   Am   G
I'm learning to fly   (Learning to fly.) but I ain't got wings. (Learning to fly.)

F   C   Am   G   F   C   Am   G
Coming down (Learning to fly.) is the hardest thing. (Learning to fly.)

GUITAR SOLO

```
            1., 2., 3.                        4.
‖: F      C      | Am      G        :‖ Am      G
```

VERSE 3

```
        F      C   Am    G    F      C    Am    G
Well, some say life            will beat you down,

  F        C    Am   G    F        C      Am    G
break your heart,            steal your crown.

          F      C    Am   G  F       C       Am     G
So, I've started out            for God-knows-where.

  F        C   Am    G     F   C    Am    G
I guess I'll know          when I get there.
```

CHORUS 3

```
        F      C   Am    G    F      C    Am     G
I'm learning to fly            around the clouds.

  F         C    Am       G    F       C     Am     G
What goes up     (Learning to fly.)   must come down.
```

INTERLUDE

```
| F      C        | Am      G        | F      C        | Am      G
        Shouted: Ay!
```

CHORUS 4

```
        F        C    Am       G      F      C    Am     G
I'm learning to fly    (Learning to fly.) but I ain't got wings.

  F      C    Am   G    F       C     Am      G
Coming down           is the hardest thing.

        F        C    Am        G    F      C      Am     G
I'm learning to fly    (Learning to fly.) around the clouds.

  F         C    Am       G     F       C      Am     G
What goes up     (Learning to fly.)    must come down.
```

OUTRO

```
        F       C   Am       G    F    C    Am       G
I'm learning to fly.   (Learning to fly.      Learning to fly.)

        F       C   Am       G    F    C    Am       G
I'm learning to fly.   (Learning to fly.      Learning to fly.)

  F    C    Am       G    F    C    Am       G    Fade
        (Learning to fly.         Learning to fly.)
```

Melissa

Words and Music by Gregg Allman and Steve Alaimo

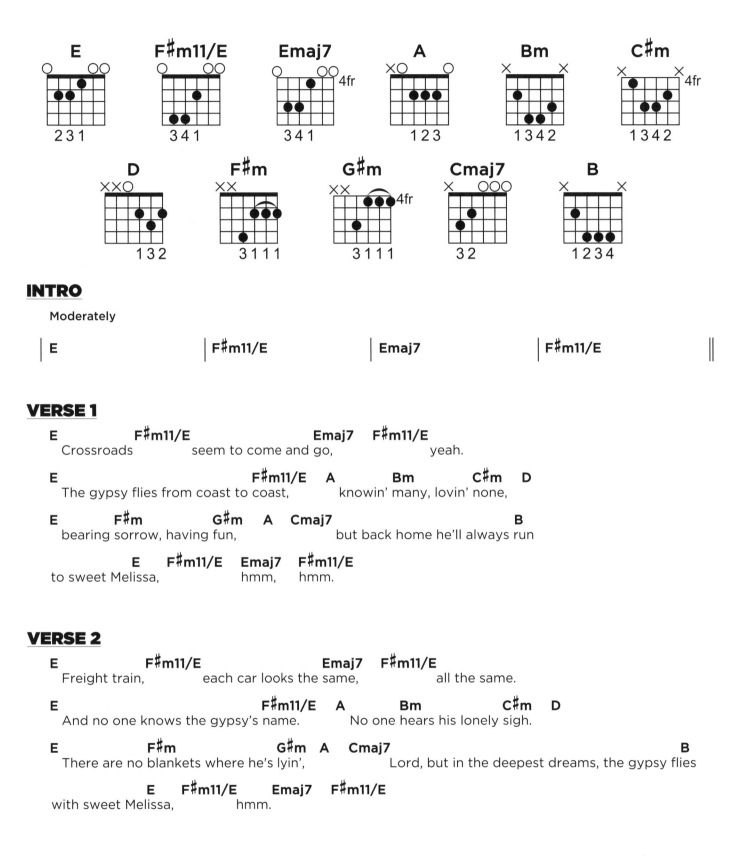

INTRO

Moderately

| E | | F#m11/E | | Emaj7 | | F#m11/E | |

VERSE 1

E   F#m11/E   Emaj7   F#m11/E
Crossroads   seem to come and go,   yeah.

E   F#m11/E   A   Bm   C#m   D
The gypsy flies from coast to coast,   knowin' many, lovin' none,

E   F#m   G#m A Cmaj7   B
bearing sorrow, having fun,   but back home he'll always run

        E   F#m11/E   Emaj7   F#m11/E
to sweet Melissa,   hmm,   hmm.

VERSE 2

E   F#m11/E   Emaj7   F#m11/E
Freight train,   each car looks the same,   all the same.

E   F#m11/E   A   Bm   C#m   D
And no one knows the gypsy's name.   No one hears his lonely sigh.

E   F#m   G#m A Cmaj7   B
There are no blankets where he's lyin',   Lord, but in the deepest dreams, the gypsy flies

        E   F#m11/E   Emaj7   F#m11/E
with sweet Melissa,   hmm.

BRIDGE

E   D
Again the mornin's come,   again he's on the run.

A   B
Sunbeams shinin' through his hair.   Better not to have a care,

C#m   A   B
so pick up your gear and, gypsy, roll on,   roll on.

VERSE 3

E   F#m11/E   Emaj7   F#m11/E
Crossroads   will you ever let him   go,   no, no, no,

E   F#m11/E A   Bm C#m   D
or will you hide the dead man's ghost?   Lord, or will he lie beneath the plain,

E   F#m   G#m   A Cmaj7   B
or will his spirit fall   away?   But I know that he won't stay

                 E   F#m11/E   Cmaj7   B
without Melissa.   Yes, I know that he won't stay, yeah,

OUTRO

                 E   F#m11/E   Emaj7   F#m11/E
without Melissa.   No, no,   just won't stay.

Repeat and fade

‖: E | F#m11/E | Emaj7 | F#m11/E   :‖

Night Moves

Words and Music by Bob Seger

(Capo 1st Fret)

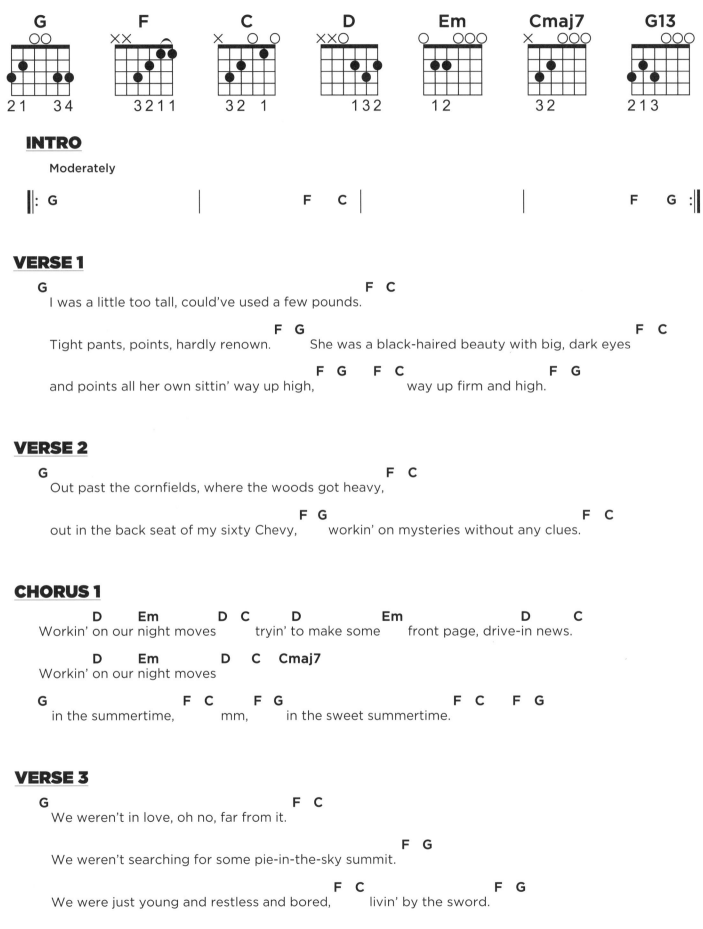

INTRO

Moderately

‖: G | F C | | F G :‖

VERSE 1

G   F C
I was a little too tall, could've used a few pounds.

                        F G   F C
Tight pants, points, hardly renown.   She was a black-haired beauty with big, dark eyes

                       F G F C   F G
and points all her own sittin' way up high,   way up firm and high.

VERSE 2

G   F C
Out past the cornfields, where the woods got heavy,

                       F G   F C
out in the back seat of my sixty Chevy,   workin' on mysteries without any clues.

CHORUS 1

        D   Em   D C   D   Em   D   C
Workin' on our night moves   tryin' to make some   front page, drive-in news.

        D   Em   D C Cmaj7
Workin' on our night moves

G   F C F G   F C F G
in the summertime,   mm,   in the sweet summertime.

VERSE 3

G   F C
We weren't in love, oh no, far from it.

We weren't searching for some pie-in-the-sky summit.   F G

                                       F C   F G
We were just young and restless and bored,   livin' by the sword.

VERSE 4

G   F   C

And we'd steal away every chance we could

                                                  F   G

to the back room, to the alley, or the trusty woods.

                                    F   C

I used her, she used me, but neither one cared.   We were gettin' our share.

CHORUS 2

        D   Em   D   C   D   Em   D   C

Workin' on our night moves   tryin' to lose those   awkward teenage blues.

        D   Em   D   C   Cmaj7

Workin' on our night moves.   Mm,

G   F   C   F G   F   C   D

and it was summertime,   mm,   sweet summertime, summertime.

INTERLUDE

| Em | | D | G | G13 |

BRIDGE

     Cmaj7   G

And oh,   the wonder

Cmaj7   F   D   G

We felt the lightning, yeah,   and we waited on the thunder,   waited on the thunder.

VERSE 5

G   Cmaj7

I awoke last night to the sound of thunder.   How far off, I sat and wondered.

G   Cmaj7

Started humming a song from nineteen sixty-two.   Ain't it funny how the night

Em   C

moves   when you just don't seem to have

Em   C   Em   C   Cmaj7   G

as much to lose?   Strange how the night moves   with autumn closing in.

REPEAT INTRO

OUTRO

w/ Lead Voc. ad. lib.

Repeat and fade

‖: G | F   C | | F   G :‖

(Night Moves.)   Night Moves.)

Patience

Words and Music by W. Axl Rose, Slash, Izzy Stradlin', Duff McKagan and Steven Adler

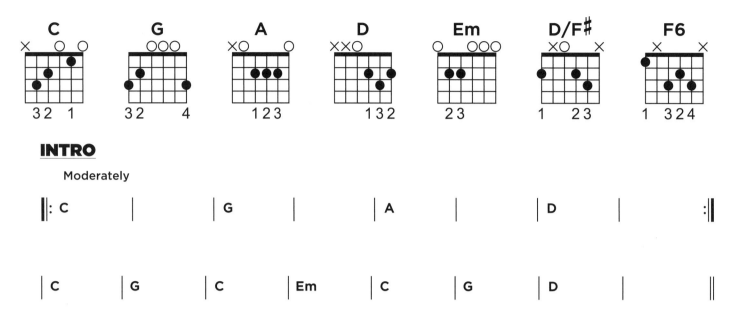

INTRO

Moderately

‖: C | | G | | A | | D | :‖

| C | G | C | Em C | G | D | ‖

VERSE 1

  C   G
    Shed a tear 'cause I'm missing you,   I'm still alright to smile.

  A   D
    Girl, I think about you ev'ry day now.

  C   G
    Was a time when I wasn't sure, but you set my mind at ease.

  A   D
    There is no doubt you're in my heart now.

CHORUS 1

  C   G   C   Em
    Said, "Woman, take it slow, it'll work itself out fine.

  C   G   D
    All we need is just a little patience."

  C   G   C   Em
    Said, "Sugar, make it slow and we come together fine.

  C   G
    All we need is just a little pa -

| D | | | | |
    tience."   Whispered: Pa - tience.

| | | | | ‖
            Mm,   yeah.

VERSE 2

C   G
I sit here on the stairs 'cause I'd   rather be alone.

   A   D
If I can't have you right now, I'll wait, dear.

C   G
Sometimes I get so tense, but I can't speed up the time.

   A   D
But you know, love, there's one more thing to consider.

CHORUS 2

C   G   C   Em
Said, "Woman, take it slow, and things will be just fine.

C   G   D
You and I'll just use a little patience."

C   G   C   Em
Said, "Sugar, take the time 'cause the lights are shining bright.

C   G
You and I've got what it takes to make

D				
it.		We won't fake it,	ah,	I'll never
break it,		'cause I can't take it."		

GUITAR SOLO

Play 3 times

‖: C | G | C | Em | C | G | D | :‖: | :‖

OUTRO

Slow

D	D/F♯	G		D	D/F♯	G	

D D/F♯   G   D   D/F♯   G
      Little patience, mm, yeah, yeah, yeah,   mm, yeah.

         D   D/F♯ G   D   D/F♯ G
Need a little patience, yeah,   just a little patience, yeah.

                                                  (Some more pa -

D   D/F♯   G
   I   been walkin' the streets   at night   just tryin' to get it right.
tience,   yeah.   Need some pa -

D   D/F♯   G
   Hard to see with so many around, you know I don't like being stuck in the crowd,   and   the
tience,   yeah.   Could use some pa -

D   D/F♯   G
streets don't change but, baby, the name.   I ain't got time for the game   'cause I   need
       tience,   yeah.   Gotta   have   some

D   D/F♯   G
   you,   yeah, yeah, but I need   you. Oo,   I   need
patience,   yeah.   All it takes is pa -

F6   G   D
   you,   whoa,   I need   you,   oo,   this   time. Whispered: Ah.
   tience,   just a little   patience   is all you need.)

Redemption Song

Words and Music by Bob Marley

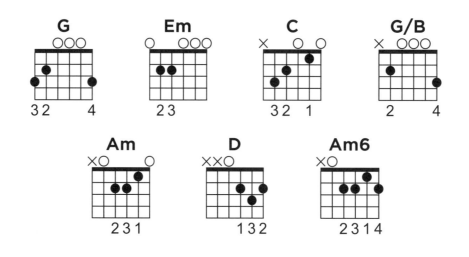

INTRO

Moderately

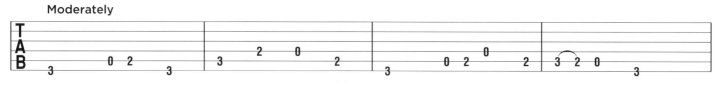

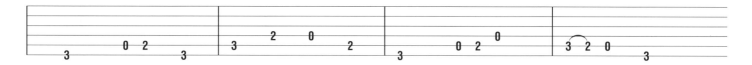

VERSE 1

G   Em C   G/B   Am
Old pirates, yes, they rob I, sold I to the merchant ships

G   Em C   G/B   Am
minutes after they took I   from the bottomless   pit.

G   Em   C   G/B   Am
But my hand was made strong   by the hand of the Almighty.

G   Em   C   D
We forward in this generation,   triumphantly.

CHORUS 1

               G C   D   G   C D
Won't you help to sing   these songs of   freedom? 'Cause all I ever have,

Em C D   G   C D   G   C D
    redemption   songs,   redemption   songs.

VERSE 2

```
        G                      Em                        C        G/B       Am
Emancipate yourselves from mental     slavery. None but ourselves can free our minds.

        G              Em              C      G/B      D
Have no fear for atomic energy 'cause none of them can stop the time.

        G                  Em           C      G/B     Am
How long shall they kill our prophets while we stand aside and look? Oo.

    G            Em          C      G/B     D
Some say it's just a part of it, we've got to fulfill the Book.
```

CHORUS 2

```
                    G   C      D        G            C  D
Won't you help to sing     these   songs of   freedom? 'Cause all I ever have,

Em  C   D     G       C   D     G       C   D     G       C   D
    redemption   songs,    redemption   songs,    redemption   songs.
```

INTERLUDE 1

```
                          1., 2., 3.                    4.
||: Em              :|        C       D      :||        C       D
```

REPEAT VERSE 2

CHORUS 3

```
                    G   C      D        G            C  D
Won't you help to sing     these   songs of   freedom? 'Cause all I ever have,

Em  C   D     G       C   D
    redemption   songs. All I ever have,

Em  C   D     Em        C      D
    redemption    songs,    these    songs of

G       C   D        G   C   G/B
freedom.     Songs of freedom.
```

OUTRO

```
| Am              |                 | Am6              |              ||
```

Tangled Up in Blue

Words and Music by Bob Dylan

A   Asus4   G/A   D   E   F#m   G

INTRO

Moderately

| A   Asus4 | A   Asus4 | A   Asus4 | A   Asus4 ‖

VERSE 1

A   G/A   A   G/A
Early one mornin' the sun was shinin', I was layin' in bed,

A   G/A   D
wond'rin' if she's changed at all, if her hair was still red.

A   G/A   A   G/A
Her folks, they said our lives together sure was gonna be rough,

A   G/A   D
they never did like Mama's homemade dress, Papa's bankbook wasn't big enough.

E   F#m   A   D
And I was standin' on the side of the road, rain fallin' on my shoes,

E   F#m   A   D   E
Heading up for the East Coast, Lord knows I've paid some dues gettin' through

G   D   A Asus4 A Asus4 A Asus4 A Asus4
tangled up in blue.

VERSE 2

A   G/A   A   G/A
She was married when we first met,   soon to be divorced,

A   G/A   D
I helped her out of a jam, I guess, but I used a little too much force.

A   G/A   A   G/A
We drove that car as far as we could, abandoned it out West,

A   G/A   D
split up on a dark, sad night, both agreeing it was best.

E   F#m   A   D
She turned around to look at me as I   was walkin' away,

E   F#m   A   D   E
I heard her say over my shoulder, "We'll meet again someday on the avenue,"

G   D   A Asus4 A Asus4 A Asus4 A Asus4
tangled up in blue.

VERSE 3

```
A              G/A              A                    G/A
I had a job in the great north woods, working as a cook for a spell.

      A             G/A            D
But I never did like it all      that much and one day the axe just fell.

      A            G/A              A                    G/A
So, I drifted down to New Orleans where I lucky was to be employed.

A                    G/A            D
Workin' for a while on a fishin' boat right outside of Delacroix.

      E         F#m           A             D
But all the while I was alone, the past was close behind.

E                     F#m          A                     D
I seen a lot of women,       but she never escaped my mind, and I just

E      G        D      A   Asus4  A   Asus4  A   Asus4  A   Asus4
grew tangled up in blue.
```

VERSE 4

```
A              G/A              A                    G/A
She was workin' in a topless place and I   stopped in for a beer.

   A              G/A                D
I just kept lookin' at the side of her face in the spotlight so clear.

      A              G/A              A                    G/A
And later on when the crowd thinned out, I's just about do the same.

         A         G/A             D
She was standing there in back of my chair, said to me, "Don't I know your name?"

   E                       F#m          A                     D
I   muttered something underneath my breath, she studied the lines on my face.

E                 F#m             A             D             E
I must admit I felt a little uneasy when she bent down to tie the laces of my shoe;

G        D        A   Asus4  A   Asus4  A   Asus4  A   Asus4
tangled up in blue.
```

VERSE 5

```
A              G/A              A             G/A
She lit a burner on the stove and offered me a pipe.

   A                        G/A             D
"I thought you'd never say hello," she said, "You look like the silent type."

        A          G/A              A             G/A
Then she opened up a book of poems and handed it to me,

A          G/A                D
written by an Italian poet from the thirteenth century.

      E                 F#m               A             D
And every one of them words rang true and glowed like burning coal.

E          F#m             A             D             E
Pouring off of every page like it was    written in my soul from me to you,

G        D        A   Asus4  A   Asus4  A   Asus4  A   Asus4
tangled up in blue.
```

VERSE 6

```
     A              G/A           A                   G/A
I lived with them on Montague Street in a basement down the stairs.

        A         G/A              D
There was music in the cafés at night and revolution in the air.

      A           G/A              A                        G/A
Then he started into dealing with slaves and something inside of him died.

  A             G/A            D
She had to sell everything she owned and    froze up inside,

     E              F♯m            A             D
And when it finally, the bottom fell out I    became withdrawn.

     E              F♯m            A                 D
The only thing I knew how to do was to keep on keepin' on    like a bird that

E    G      D      A   Asus4  A  Asus4  A  Asus4  A  Asus4
flew tangled up in blue.
```

VERSE 7

```
     A          G/A              A           G/A
So, now I'm goin' back again, I got to get her somehow.

  A             G/A                   D
All the people we used to know, they're an illusion to me now..

  A               G/A   A              G/A
Some are mathematicians; some are carpenter's wives.

      A             G/A            D
Don't know how it all got started, I don't know what they're doin' with their lives.

    E          F♯m        A              D
But me, I'm still on the road, headin' for another joint.

  E           F♯m             A                 D          E
We always did feel the same, we just saw it from a different point of view

G         D        A   Asus4  A  Asus4  A  Asus4  A  Asus4
tangled up in blue.
```

OUTRO

```
| A        G/A    | A        G/A    | A        G/A    | D                    |

| A        G/A    | A        G/A    | A        G/A    | D                    |

| E     F♯m       | A     D         | E     F♯m       | A        D           |

| E               |        G      D | A               |                      ||
```

Uncle John's Band

Words by Robert Hunter
Music by Jerry Garcia

G   Bm7   C   D

Am   Em   Dm   Dsus2

INTRO

Moderately fast

| G | | | | |
| Bm7   C | D | G   Bm7   C | D |

VERSE 1

G   C   G
Well, the first days are the hardest days, don't you worry anymore.

                            C   G
'Cause when life looks like Easy Street, there is danger at your door.

Am   Em C   D
Think this through with me.   Let me know your mind.

C D G   D C G D   G
Whoa, oh, what I want to know   is are you kind?

VERSE 2

G   C   G
It's a buck dancer's choice, my friends, better take my advice.

                       C   G
You know all the rules by now and the fire from the ice.

Am   Em C   D
Will you come with me?   Won't you come with me?

C D G   D C G D   G
Whoa, oh, what I want to know: will you come with me?

CHORUS 1

G   C   Am   G   D
God damn, well, I declare,   have you seen the like?

         C   G   D   C   D
Their walls are built of cannonballs. Their motto is, "Don't tread on me?"

G   C   Am   G   D
Come hear Uncle John's Band playing to the tide.

C   G   D   C   D
Come with me or go alone, he's come to take his children home.

GUITAR SOLO

                           1., 2., 3.   4.

‖: G   Bm7   C | D   :‖   D

VERSE 3

    G   C   G
It's   the same story the crow told me; it's the only one he knows.

                                       C   G
Like the morning sun you come and like the wind you go.

Am   Em   C   D
Ain't no time to hate,   barely time to wait,

C   D   G   D   C   G   D   G
Whoa, oh, what I want to know: where does the time go?

VERSE 4

G   C   G
 I live in a silver mine and I call it Beggar's Tomb.

                          C   G
I got me a violin and I beg you call the tune.

Am   Em   C   D
Anybody's choice;   I can hear your voice.

C   D   G   D   C   G   D   G
Whoa, oh, what I want to know: how does the song go?

CHORUS 2

G   C   Am   G   D
Come hear Uncle John's Band by the riverside.

C   G   D   C   D
Got some things to talk about, here beside the risin' tide.

G   C   Am   G   D
 Come hear Uncle John's Band playing to the tide.

C   G   D   C   D
Come on along or go alone, he's come to take his children home.

INTERLUDE

‖: Dm | G   C   :‖ Dsus2 | |

                                             C   G

Whoa, oh, what I want to know: how does the song go?

REPEAT CHORUS 2

OUTRO

Dm   **G**   **C**

       Da, da, da, da, da,

Dm   **G**   **C**

da.   Da, da, da, da, da,

Dm   **G**   **C**   **Dsus2**

da.   Da, da, da, da, da, da.

Time in a Bottle

Words and Music by Jim Croce

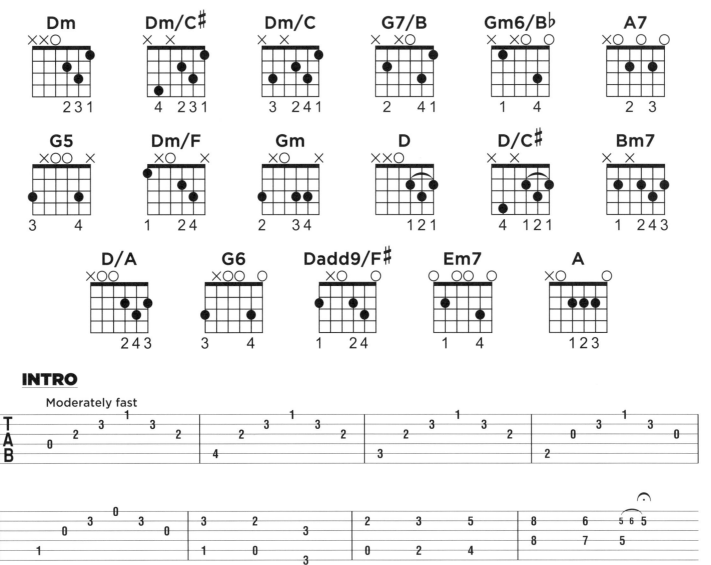

INTRO

Moderately fast

VERSE 1

Dm	Dm/C♯		Dm/C	G7/B	Gm6/B♭		A7

If I could save   time in a bottle,   the first thing that I'd like to do

Dm	Dm/C	Gm6/B♭	G5	Dm/F		Gm

is to save everyday 'til eternity passes away,   just to spend them with you.

VERSE 2

Dm	Dm/C♯	Dm/C	G7/B	Gm6/B♭		A7
If I could make days last forever,				if words could make wishes come true,		

Dm	Dm/C	Gm6/B♭	G5	Dm/F	Gm
I'd save everyday like a treasure and then			again, I would spend them with you.		

But there

BRIDGE

D	D/C♯	Bm7	D/A
never seems to be enough time to do the things you want to do once you			

G6	Dadd9/F♯	Em7	A
find them.			

D	D/C♯	Bm7	D/A
I've looked around enough to know that you're the one I want to go through			

G6	Dadd9/F♯	Em7	A
time with.			

REPEAT INTRO

VERSE 3

Dm	Dm/C♯	Dm/C	G7/B	Gm6/B♭	A7
If I had a box just for wishes		and dreams that had never come true,			

Dm	Dm/C	Gm6/B♭	G5	Dm/F	Gm
the box would be empty except for the memory of how they were answered by you.					

But there

REPEAT BRIDGE

OUTRO

Play 3 times

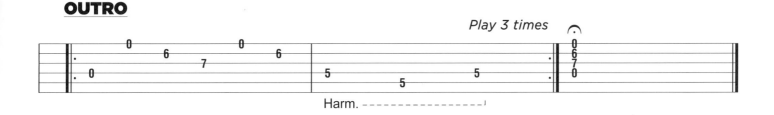

Harm.

Wild World

Words and Music by Cat Stevens

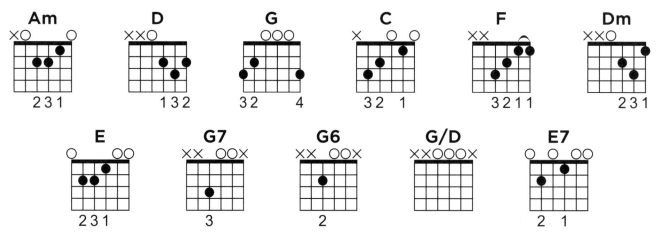

INTRO

Moderately slow

Am   D   G   C
    La, la, la, la, la, la, la, la, la, la.   La, la, la, la, la, la, la, la, la, la.

F   Dm   E
    La, la, la, la, la, la, la, la, la, la, la, la.

VERSE 1

Am   D   G   C
    Now that I've lost everything to you, you say you want to start something

F   Dm   E
new, and it's breakin' my heart you're leavin'. Baby, I'm grievin'.

Am   D   G   C
    But if you want to leave, take good care. Hope you have a lot of nice things to wear,

F   Dm   E   G G7 G6 G/D
but then a lot of nice things turn bad out there.

CHORUS 1

C   G   F
    Oo, baby, baby, it's a wild world.

G   F   C
    It's hard to get by   just upon a smile.

G   F
    Oo, baby, baby, it's a wild world.

G   F   C   Dm E7
    I'll always remember you like a child, girl.

VERSE 2

```
Am                       D                    G      C
      You know I've seen a lot of what the world can do and it's breakin' my heart in

F          Dm                    E
two because I never want to see you sad, girl. Don't be a bad girl.

Am                   D           G                      C
      But if you want to leave, take good care. Hope you make a lot of nice friends out

F              Dm                         E     G    G7  G6  G/D
there, but just remember there's a lot of bad, and beware.
```

CHORUS 2

```
C     G            F
   Oo, baby, baby, it's a wild world.

G                 F          C
   It's hard to get by    just upon a smile.

      G             F
   Oo, baby, baby, it's a wild world.

N.C.       G            F            C           Dm    E7
      And I'll always remember you like a child, girl.
```

INTERLUDE

```
Am   D   G        C
            La, la, la, la, la, la, la, la, la, la.

F            Dm              E
   La, la, la, la, la, la, la, la, la, la, la, la. Baby, I love you.
```

VERSE 3

```
Am                   D           G                      C
      But if you want to leave, take good care. Hope you make a lot of nice friends out

F              Dm                         E     G    G7  G6  G/D
there, but just remember there's a lot of bad, and beware.
```

REPEAT CHORUS 2

CHORUS 3

```
C     G            F
   Oo, baby, baby, it's a wild world.

G                 F          C
   It's hard to get by    just upon a smile.

      G             F
   Oo, baby, baby, it's a wild world.

N.C.       G            F            C
      And I'll always remember you like a child, girl.
```

Wanted Dead or Alive

Words and Music by Jon Bon Jovi and Richie Sambora

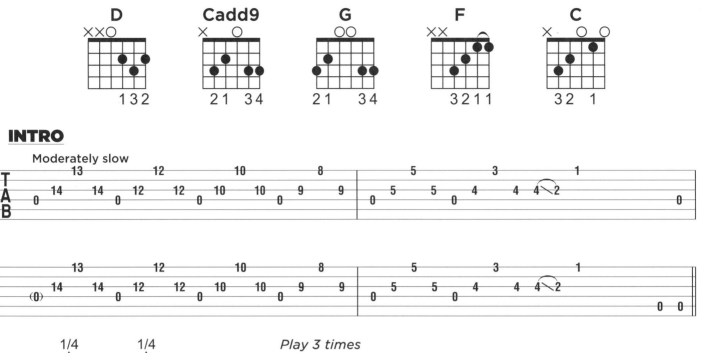

INTRO

Moderately slow

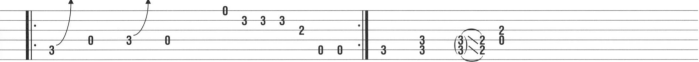

Play 3 times

VERSE 1

D   **Cadd9**   **G**
It's all the same, only the names will change.

Cadd9 **G**   **F** **D**
Every day   it seems we're wasting away.

               Cadd9   **G**
Another place, where the faces are so   cold,

Cadd9 **G**   **F** **D**
I'd drive all night just to get back home.

CHORUS 1

     C   **G**   **F**   **D**
I'm a cowboy,   on a steel horse I   ride. I'm

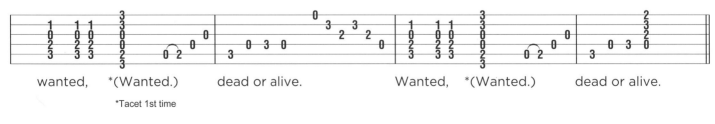

wanted, *(Wanted.)   dead or alive.   Wanted, *(Wanted.)   dead or alive.

*Tacet 1st time

INTERLUDE

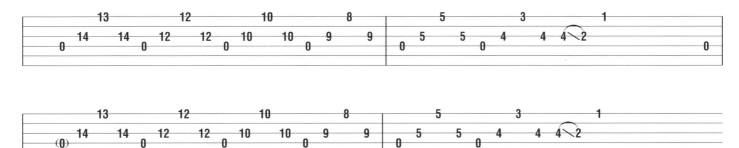

VERSE 2

      D   **Cadd9**   **G**
Sometimes I sleep, sometimes it's not for days.

   Cadd9   **G**   **F**   **D**
The people I meet   always go their sep'rate ways.

                         Cadd9   **G**
Sometimes you tell the day by the bottle that you   drink.

   Cadd9   **G**   **F**   **D**
And times when you're alone all you do is think.

REPEAT CHORUS 1

REPEAT INTERLUDE

GUITAR SOLO

||: D | Cadd9 G | Cadd9 G | F D :|| F D

1.   2.

CHORUS 2

     C   **G**   **F**   **D**   **C**   **G**
I'm a cowboy,   on a steel horse I   ride. I'm wanted, (Wanted.)

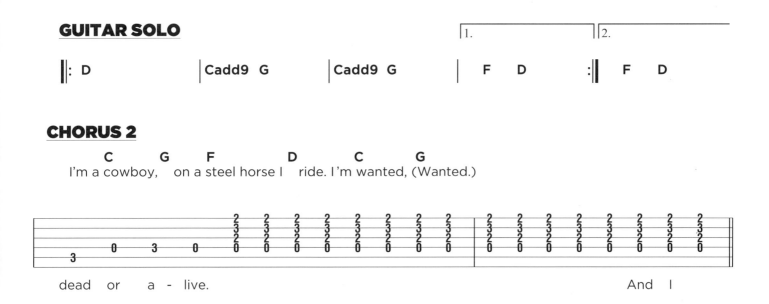

dead   or   a - live.   And I

VERSE 3

D   **Cadd9**   **G**
walk these streets, a loaded six string on my   back.

Cadd9   **G**   **F**   **D**
I play for keeps   'cause I might not make it back.

                                      Cadd9   **G**
I've been ev'rywhere, still I'm standing tall,

      Cadd9   **G**   **F**   **D**
I've seen a million faces, and I've rocked them all.

CHORUS 3

              C   **G**   **F**   **D**
'Cause I'm a cowboy,   on a steel horse I   ride. I'm

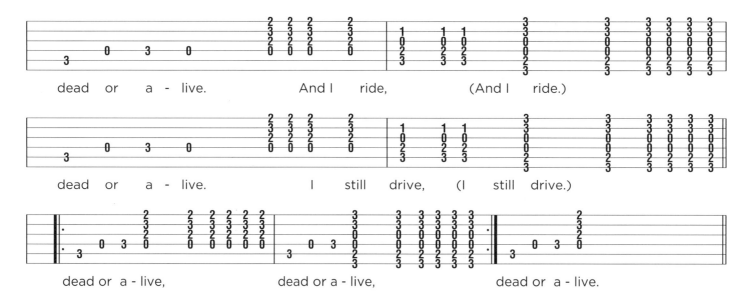

wanted,   (Wanted.)   dead   or   a - live.   'Cause I'm a

C   **G**   **F**   **D**   **C**   **G**
cowboy,   I got the night on my side. And I'm wanted, (Wanted.)

dead   or   a - live.   And I   ride,   (And I   ride.)

dead   or   a - live.   I   still drive,   (I   still drive.)

dead or a - live,   dead or a - live,   dead or a - live.

OUTRO

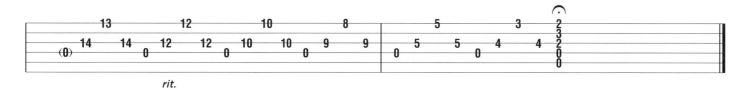

rit.

REALLY EASY GUITAR

Easy-to-follow charts to get you playing right away are presented in these collections of arrangements in chords, lyrics and basic tab for all guitarists.

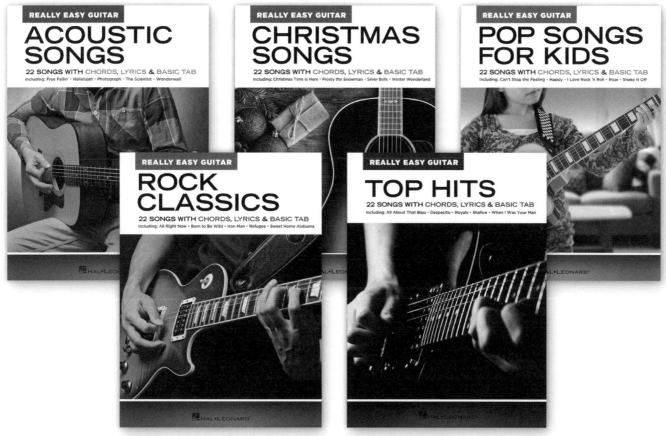

ACOUSTIC CLASSICS

22 songs: Angie • Best of My Love • Dust in the Wind • Fire and Rain • A Horse with No Name • Layla • More Than a Feeling • Night Moves • Patience • Time in a Bottle • Wanted Dead or Alive • and more.
00300600 ....$9.99

ACOUSTIC SONGS

22 songs: Free Fallin' • Good Riddance (Time of Your Life) • Hallelujah • I'm Yours • Losing My Religion • Mr. Jones • Photograph • Riptide • The Scientist • Wonderwall • and more.
00286663 ....$9.99

THE BEATLES FOR KIDS

14 songs: All You Need Is Love • Blackbird • Good Day Sunshine • Here Comes the Sun • I Want to Hold Your Hand • Let It Be • With a Little Help from My Friends • Yellow Submarine • and more.
00346031 ....$9.99

CHRISTMAS CLASSICS

22 Christmas carols: Away in a Manger • Deck the Hall • It Came upon the Midnight Clear • Jingle Bells • Silent Night • The Twelve Days of Christmas • We Wish You a Merry Christmas • and more.
00348327 ....$9.99

CHRISTMAS SONGS

22 holiday favorites: Blue Christmas • Christmas Time Is Here • Frosty the Snowman • Have Yourself a Merry Little Christmas • Mary, Did You Know? • Silver Bells • Winter Wonderland • and more.
00294775 ....$9.99

THE DOORS

22 songs: Break on Through to the Other Side • Hello, I Love You (Won't You Tell Me Your Name?) • L.A. Woman • Light My Fire • Love Her Madly • People Are Strange • Riders on the Storm • Touch Me • and more.
00345890 ....$9.99

BILLIE EILISH

14 songs: All the Good Girls Go to Hell • Bad Guy • Everything I Wanted • Idontwannabeyouanymore • No Time to Die • Ocean Eyes • Six Feet Under • Wish You Were Gay • and more.
00346351 ....$9.99

POP SONGS FOR KIDS

22 songs: Brave • Can't Stop the Feeling • Happy • I Love Rock 'N Roll • Let It Go • Roar • Shake It Off • We Got the Beat • and more.
00286698 ....$9.99

ROCK CLASSICS

22 songs: All Right Now • Born to Be Wild • Don't Fear the Reaper • Hey Joe • Iron Man • Old Time Rock & Roll • Refugee • Sweet Home Alabama • You Shook Me All Night Long • and more.
00286699 ....$9.99

TOP HITS

22 hits: All About That Bass • All of Me • Despacito • Love Yourself • Royals • Say Something • Shallow • Someone like You • This Is Me • A Thousand Years • When I Was Your Man • and more.
00300599 ....$9.99

halleonard.com

EASY GUITAR
WITH NOTES & TAB

This series features simplified arrangements with notes, tab, chord charts, and strum and pick patterns.

MIXED FOLIOS

00702287	Acoustic	$16.99
00702002	Acoustic Rock Hits for Easy Guitar	$15.99
00702166	All-Time Best Guitar Collection	$19.99
00702232	Best Acoustic Songs for Easy Guitar	$14.99
00119835	Best Children's Songs	$16.99
00702233	Best Hard Rock Songs	$15.99
00703055	The Big Book of Nursery Rhymes & Children's Songs	$16.99
00698978	Big Christmas Collection	$17.99
00702394	Bluegrass Songs for Easy Guitar	$12.99
00289632	Bohemian Rhapsody	$17.99
00703387	Celtic Classics	$14.99
00224808	Chart Hits of 2016-2017	$14.99
00267383	Chart Hits of 2017-2018	$14.99
00334293	Chart Hits of 2019-2020	$16.99
00702149	Children's Christian Songbook	$9.99
00702028	Christmas Classics	$8.99
00101779	Christmas Guitar	$14.99
00702185	Christmas Hits	$10.99
00702141	Classic Rock	$8.95
00159642	Classical Melodies	$12.99
00253933	Disney/Pixar's Coco	$16.99
00702203	CMT's 100 Greatest Country Songs	$29.99
00702283	The Contemporary Christian Collection	$16.99
00196954	Contemporary Disney	$19.99

00702239	Country Classics for Easy Guitar	$22.99
00702257	Easy Acoustic Guitar Songs	$14.99
00702280	Easy Guitar Tab White Pages	$29.99
00702041	Favorite Hymns for Easy Guitar	$10.99
00222701	Folk Pop Songs	$14.99
00126894	Frozen	$14.99
00333922	Frozen 2	$14.99
00702286	Glee	$16.99
00702160	The Great American Country Songbook	$16.99
00267383	Great American Gospel for Guitar	$12.99
00702050	Great Classical Themes for Easy Guitar	$8.99
00702116	Greatest Hymns for Guitar	$10.99
00275088	The Greatest Showman	$17.99
00148030	Halloween Guitar Songs	$14.99
00702273	Irish Songs	$12.99
00192503	Jazz Classics for Easy Guitar	$14.99
00702275	Jazz Favorites for Easy Guitar	$15.99
00702274	Jazz Standards for Easy Guitar	$17.99
00702162	Jumbo Easy Guitar Songbook	$19.99
00232285	La La Land	$16.99
00702258	Legends of Rock	$14.99
00702189	MTV's 100 Greatest Pop Songs	$24.95
00702272	1950s Rock	$15.99
00702271	1960s Rock	$15.99
00702270	1970s Rock	$16.99
00702269	1980s Rock	$15.99

00702268	1990s Rock	$19.99
00109725	Once	$14.99
00702187	Selections from O Brother Where Art Thou?	$19.99
00702178	100 Songs for Kids	$14.99
00702515	Pirates of the Caribbean	$16.99
00702125	Praise and Worship for Guitar	$10.99
00287930	Songs from *A Star Is Born, The Greatest Showman, La La Land*, and More Movie Musicals	$16.99
00702285	Southern Rock Hits	$12.99
00156420	Star Wars Music	$14.99
00121535	30 Easy Celtic Guitar Solos	$15.99
00702156	3-Chord Rock	$12.99
00702220	Today's Country Hits	$12.99
00244654	Top Hits of 2017	$14.99
00283786	Top Hits of 2018	$14.99
00702294	Top Worship Hits	$15.99
00702255	VH1's 100 Greatest Hard Rock Songs	$29.99
00702175	VH1's 100 Greatest Songs of Rock and Roll	$27.99
00702253	Wicked	$12.99

ARTIST COLLECTIONS

00702267	AC/DC for Easy Guitar	$15.99
00702598	Adele for Easy Guitar	$15.99
00156221	Adele – 25	$16.99
00702040	Best of the Allman Brothers	$16.99
00702865	J.S. Bach for Easy Guitar	$14.99
00702169	Best of The Beach Boys	$12.99
00702292	The Beatles — 1	$19.99
00125796	Best of Chuck Berry	$15.99
00702201	The Essential Black Sabbath	$12.95
00702250	blink-182 — Greatest Hits	$16.99
02501615	Zac Brown Band — The Foundation	$19.99
02501621	Zac Brown Band — You Get What You Give	$16.99
00702043	Best of Johnny Cash	$16.99
00702090	Eric Clapton's Best	$12.99
00702086	Eric Clapton — from the Album Unplugged	$15.99
00702202	The Essential Eric Clapton	$15.99
00702053	Best of Patsy Cline	$15.99
00222697	Very Best of Coldplay – 2nd Edition	$14.99
00702229	The Very Best of Creedence Clearwater Revival	$15.99
00702145	Best of Jim Croce	$15.99
00702219	David Crowder*Band Collection	$12.95
00702278	Crosby, Stills & Nash	$12.99
14042809	Bob Dylan	$14.99
00702276	Fleetwood Mac — Easy Guitar Collection	$16.99
00139462	The Very Best of Grateful Dead	$15.99
00702136	Best of Merle Haggard	$14.99
00702227	Jimi Hendrix — Smash Hits	$19.99
00702288	Best of Hillsong United	$12.99
00702236	Best of Antonio Carlos Jobim	$15.99

00702245	Elton John — Greatest Hits 1970–2002	$17.99
00129855	Jack Johnson	$16.99
00702204	Robert Johnson	$12.99
00702234	Selections from Toby Keith — 35 Biggest Hits	$12.95
00702003	Kiss	$16.99
00110578	Best of Kutless	$12.99
00702216	Lynyrd Skynyrd	$16.99
00702182	The Essential Bob Marley	$14.99
00146081	Maroon 5	$14.99
00121925	Bruno Mars – Unorthodox Jukebox	$12.99
00702248	Paul McCartney — All the Best	$14.99
00702129	Songs of Sarah McLachlan	$12.95
00125484	The Best of MercyMe	$12.99
02501316	Metallica — Death Magnetic	$19.99
00702209	Steve Miller Band — Young Hearts (Greatest Hits)	$12.95
00124167	Jason Mraz	$15.99
00702096	Best of Nirvana	$15.99
00702211	The Offspring — Greatest Hits	$12.95
00138026	One Direction	$14.99
00702030	Best of Roy Orbison	$16.99
00702144	Best of Ozzy Osbourne	$14.99
00702279	Tom Petty	$12.99
00102911	Pink Floyd	$16.99
00702139	Elvis Country Favorites	$17.99
00702293	The Very Best of Prince	$16.99
00699415	Best of Queen for Guitar	$15.99
00109279	Best of R.E.M.	$14.99
00702208	Red Hot Chili Peppers — Greatest Hits	$16.99
00198960	The Rolling Stones	$16.99
00174793	The Very Best of Santana	$14.99
00702196	Best of Bob Seger	$15.99

00146046	Ed Sheeran	$17.99
00702252	Frank Sinatra — Nothing But the Best	$17.99
00702010	Best of Rod Stewart	$16.99
00702049	Best of George Strait	$14.99
00702259	Taylor Swift for Easy Guitar	$15.99
00254499	Taylor Swift – Easy Guitar Anthology	$19.99
00702260	Taylor Swift — Fearless	$14.99
00139727	Taylor Swift — 1989	$17.99
00115960	Taylor Swift — Red	$16.99
00253667	Taylor Swift — Reputation	$17.99
00702290	Taylor Swift — Speak Now	$16.99
00702223	Chris Tomlin—Arriving	$16.99
00232849	Chris Tomlin Collection – 2nd Edition	$12.95
00702226	Chris Tomlin — See the Morning	$12.95
00148643	Train	$14.99
00702427	U2 — 18 Singles	$16.99
00702108	Best of Stevie Ray Vaughan	$16.99
00279005	The Who	$14.99
00702123	Best of Hank Williams	$15.99
00194548	Best of John Williams	$14.99
00702111	Stevie Wonder — Guitar Collection	$9.95
00702228	Neil Young — Greatest Hits	$15.99
00119133	Neil Young — Harvest	$14.99

Prices, contents and availability
subject to change without notice.

HAL•LEONARD®

Visit Hal Leonard online at **halleonard.com**

0720

306